American Daughters

American Daughters

Poems by

VA Smith

© 2023 VA Smith. All rights reserved.
This material may not be reproduced in any form, published,
reprinted, recorded, performed, broadcast,
rewritten, or redistributed without
the explicit permission of VA Smith.
All such actions are strictly prohibited by law.

Cover design by Shay Culligan
Cover art by iStock Photos

ISBN: 978-1-63980-245-6

Kelsay Books
502 South 1040 East, A-119
American Fork, Utah 84003
Kelsaybooks.com

For all my sisters—the many women who have led me
& those who have inspired these poems.

Acknowledgments

I thank the editors of the following publications in which these poems, some in different forms, first appeared:

Around the World: Landscapes and City Scapes/Anthology:
   "Hiking: Taos, New Mexico,"
   published under the title "Black Hills, South Dakota"

Blue Lake Review: "Caroline at 69"

Calyx Journal: "Interstices"

Feels Blind Literary: "After the Fire," "My Future Memory"

Ginosko Literary Journal: "Adoption," "Are We There Yet?"
   "Come on Down"

MacQueen's Quinterly: "The Idea of Order in Idaho,"
   published under the title "The Idea of Order in South Jersey,"
   "No Country for Young Lawyers," "Treatment Aria"

Oyster River Pages: "Polyamory"

Pure Slush/Work: "Millennial Cowgirl"

Rat's Ass Review: "Biker Mama Angelus"

Songs of Eretz Poetry Review: "Jersey Girl," "Orthodox Lent"

Third Wednesday: "Team Captain"

Tipton Poetry Review: "To Be Zorro"

Verdad: "The Problem That Has No Name,"
   published under the title "Cuttings"

Again—
Deep gratitude to Bill Keeney
& Mary Rohrer-Dann:
Readers who helped these lines
to sing & sway.

Contents

Preface: A Note on Not Staying in My Lane	15

I American Daughters

Flapper	19
The Problem That Has No Name	21
Home with the Death Business	23
Come on Down	25
Caroline at 69	27
Adoption	30
Motherless Child	32
Treatment Aria	35
The Idea of Order in Idaho	37
When Dumplings Open into Lotus Flowers	39
Moab Requiem	41
No Country for Young Lawyers	43
Polyamory	45
Interstices	46
A Study in Posing	47
Biker Mama Angelus	49
Millennial Cowgirl	50
Jersey Girl	52
Gold Over America Tour	54

II Team Captain & Other Poems

Team Captain	59
To Be Zorro	60
Hiking: Taos, New Mexico	63
Are We There Yet?	64
What a City Has to Offer	65
Odalisque	66
American Sonnet	68

After the Fire	69
Orthodox Lent	72
My Future Memory	74
Quarantine Cuisine	76
Ode to the Christmas Cactus	77

Preface: A Note on Not Staying in My Lane

The title *American Daughters* might wink and nod at its readers. With Part 1's chorus of voices, arranged chronologically from 1921–2021, I intend io trouble the singularity and exclusiveness of THE America, as well as to question who gets to be (U.S.) American. Additionally, I want the overdetermined term "daughters" to play with the paterfamilias myth of founding fathers and masculine privilege.

My rearing in small town Appalachia, decades as a student and teacher in Eastern universities, and life in and adjacent to Philadelphia queer cultures and communities of color, have provided a wide swath of networks, friendships, and intimacies contributing to the identities in this collection.

Organic as this inclusivity might be, I also migrate from my home culture in representing some of these speakers, stepping into the potentially problematic ethical terrain of appropriating other cultures and identities. As many of us are aware, this has become a national conversation among cultural critics, artists, public intellectuals, and journalists. Voicing other identities and stories outside of our own culture can be troubling for reasons most of us understand: 1) this appropriation might easily create demeaning or damaging stereotypes, and/or 2) culturally dominant individuals or groups steal, sometimes literally, art, voices, and stories from marginalized or underrepresented individuals or groups.

Speaking from a variety of perspectives, many writers and artists are currently conducting nuanced ethical examinations of cultural appropriation. I mention here a representative few. Poet and cultural critic Paisley Rekdal engages extensively with classroom content and wider uses of writerly cultural appropriation. Yet she also asks if cultural appropriation might add possibility to literature's project. Rekdal offers Hannah Arendt's term "compassionate approximations" as a way of thinking and writing against inauthentic cultural appropriation, aptly distilled in this question: "Does [writing in the voice of another] mute other writers we wish to speak alongside of, or does it bring more voices into this conversation?" More boldly, NYT journalist Pamela Paul writes convincingly about "the limits of lived experience," claiming "culture is a conversation, not a monologue." Henry Louis Gates, an African American, Harvard literary scholar, celebrates the freedom to read and learn and write across culture and race in search of deeper humility and humanity: "Whenever we treat an identity as something to be fenced off from those of another identity, we sell short the human imagination."

It is my hope that inhabiting poetic personas outside of my own subject position in *American Daughters* allows me to hear and speak alongside other voices in compassion and possibility. Then again, only readers can decide if this community of voices breathes with individual complexity and speaks with cultural humility in the service of joy as well as witness.

I

American Daughters

"The connections between and among women are the most feared, the most problematic, and the most potentially transforming force on the planet."

—Adrienne Rich,
"Disloyal to Civilization": Feminism, Racism, and Gynophobia

Flapper

in memoriam: Ruth Dimling Garman 1904–1977

When the gals at Grier Boarding
chatter about their mamas—
their stables, gardens, and card
clubs—I go quiet, mine gone
by my seventh birthday. Father remarried
by my ninth, then shipped me away
like an orphan in a Dickens' tale.
My brother, as well.

He and I swim and row together
Eagles' Mere summers,
the lake sparking diamonds
when I break its stormy surface
with my dive,
bathing bloomers a bother,
dragging me down, though
our stepmother insists on modesty
when she and father visit.

Yoo-hoo! Wouldn't she just have died
at us Grier girls together in Atlantic City
last weekend, taking the train, staying at
The Marlborough Blenheim Hotel, which
Dorothy's father built, fire-proof concrete
and massive, yet pretty, I must say: giant
eaves to block the sun while we lounge
on the front porch with lemonade,
curlicues galore trailing the gingerbread
facade.

And don't you know, we bought new suits
for the beach, all dark, skin-tight stretching
to our knees, the girls coaxing me to bind
my big breasts to look the fashion,

and so I did, our heads also capped in black,
posing for the camera like sleek,
wet seals.

That salt air made us new, glowing,
waiting for the barber to bob our hair,
boyish and smooth, though my curls
just popped out shorter,
not curved and carefree,
which got me to recall
my mama spiraling
finger waves down my back
before her sickness,
her gentle touch still hidden
in my body.

That night we Griers bought
meringues and taffy, watched
trapeze artists swoop over the sea,
then horses led up a ramp to jump
from the Steel Pier into the Atlantic,
the others smiling and clapping,
but me thinking how things
freeing and brave can turn us
to the open waters, forcing us
under.

The Problem That Has No Name

after Betty Friedan

When my new husband confessed
to cutting down
ten tender pink dogwoods that fall
as he cleared my parents' land
to build our house,
I could not know
how I would miss that loveliness come spring.

By April we were settled.
I curled into the cold commode
spitting up saltines and watching
blue veins brighten my white breasts
as if pulsing to the surface.

Though I roughened the nipples with a washcloth,
I could not stand the newborn's mouth
sucking my swollen skin,
so slipped
a rubber nipple between his gums.

David wailed while I rocked him and sang,
pulling his spindly, bowed legs
to his tummy in pain as I wept
and wondered why babies were drawn
asleep and smiling on pastel mounds of clouds.

When Betty Wilder returned
from college over Christmas
heavy and depressed,
we pushed my baby buggy all over Hillcrest,
bundled against the knife-like wind,
across acres of farmland stench.

The baby sleeping opened
Betty's turn to cry
and stare, her scarred-over wrists
calling out to my loneliness,
her tales of silent dates with vain boys
and hours with textbooks a wound to me.

Now I am thinking of when the budding will begin.
At night, I picture myself
in those black capris and huaraches,
smiling at the camera,
sunning my face on the front stoop
our coal-black spaniel dropping
a freshly killed baby bunny at my feet.

Home with the Death Business

I came down off that mountain at 18,
headed to nursing school in Knoxville,
oldest of five girls, Mama dead,
leaving the others to keep themselves safe
from Pap's ways.

These days all I'm nursing is myself,
89 and getting funny in the head,
damned open wound won't heal,
ankles and feet swelled up
like musk melons.

My life has cycled in and out
of this funeral home. I spend
most days dozing and remembering,
here above Fell's Memorial
where Nannie, now me, spent decades
huffing and puffing up these
winding stairs like them fairy tale
wolves. And how this house has survived.

In the 50s when we bought
this mansion, Gene fresh from
mortuary science,
we needed that space between
bereavement below and our
family life up high. We were
at home with the death business,
taught our kids not to mind when
friends called us *The Addams Family*.

Last week my mind was stuck
in the 60s when we moved
to our big split level near the farms,

me starting card club, chairing
the yearly Snowball, the kids
in Cotillion. For all we'd gained,
those years were a misery,
finding ladies' lacy panties
in my husband's car, pregnant
with my third. When I wasn't cleaning
our house I was sticking my finger
down my throat, leaving his toilet laced
with orange vomit.
What I know by now: wheel's always
turning. Gene came back to me,
my girl popular, picked Yearbook Best Body
then '72 Homecoming Queen,
long blonde hair, tiara and her white
smile shining in the dark that crisp
football night. That's the photo
her daughter and I featured
at her funeral five years back,
gone with COPD a decade after
she buried her son Sammy.
Found him cold and blue,
OD'ed in the basement.

Well, the century's turned
and here I am,
an old lady lost in my dreams
where the dead come alive
and the living go ghost,
where my lost girl and her
tow-headed babies visit Gene
and me in Florida, and then here
come my sons and sisters,
wading that warm green Gulf's
shoreline, peaceful, all home.

Come on Down

Before the Philly day wraps us
in its thick, muggy blanket, I carry
the sparrows' bag to our stoop,

even when it rains. They're already
lined up, so I sling bread cubes
across our alley, the brown birds

tussling one another, little street urchins
itching for their share, the block
still dark and hushed this early, just me,

my hot coffee and those pure bird souls
scrounging for crumbs. What my
own life has been, me and my sweet

son, God love him, living together
here these forty-five years, my tailoring
work, his Disability, lately Medicare,

Social—enough for scraping by.
I try to do that gratitude stuff magazines
preach, I do, along with that peace breathing,

and to be glad for others' gifts, such as
my little sister and her husband's cruises
each February 'cept during the COVID.

Then her showing off pictures of raw bars
and umbrella drinks saying "Rose, I am
bringing you with us next year, I mean

it!" Well, even if, who would take care
of Anthony, as I must, day in and out,
getting him to Mass, watching over

his chores and socializing—away
from kids. Well, today I am grateful for
the 50th anniversary of The Price is Right!

Lordie, I have had my fun with that show
all these decades, curling up at 15 with
my mom on our sofa in this very house,

loving on Bob Barker. Now it's me
and my boy watching. I know most
contestants just go home with a year's

supply of *Bounty,* or whatever
Drew Carey and them decide
you're worth. Still, I have my

dreams, a little filling for my bare
life. I often fall asleep to thoughts
of Anthony and me flying to

Television City, California,
us getting the price just right.

Caroline at 69

I. House and Garden
Coffee and cinnamon smells
rise like heat to my bed,
wake me for today's treatment.

Friends' food floods our house.
Neighbors leave lemon bars, key lime pies lathered in whipped
    cream,
Southern mac n' cheese, deviled eggs fill the fridge, quiches and
    casseroles
line the kitchen table. Beef tenderloins fat as forearms appear in
    foil pans,
marinating in our foyer. My sister roasts them as she folds our
    laundry.
I'm ravenous for it all.

Plant tasks soothe me.
Each week I lay ice cubes
in the orchids sent after my brain surgery.
These tropic lovelies dot the creamy parlor
with magenta moth wings. It's odd,
I guess, to worry this hothouse care
as glioblastoma gnaws quietly
on my brain.

II. My Daughter's Wedding—The Play
Oh, Susannah, your nuptials' drama
could have been staged at my Firehouse
Theatre before that Board of bored,
social climbing bitches kicked me
to the curb.
Think of the material:

Scheduling then postponing
safe dates like shifting sand
each month as COVID
policy loosened and tightened,
then a tucked in pop-up—
a terminal mother of the bride!
But who to script it?

Sarah Ruhl? Teresa Rebeck? Tom Stoppard!
Heady and a hoot, crushing the fourth wall,
you and your audience masked, doubling
as guests and "I Do Crew," a wake within
a play about a wedding that almost wasn't.
Then The Real Thing: video sequences
of me sacked out after radiation
the day before the ceremony,
my face now puffed on steroids.
Miss Piggy in pink chiffon?

The real marriage day's more dark comedy:
bridesmaids robed in French Terry
for the hair and make-up bit,
drinking Prosecco,
slipping soft rose petals into envelopes to toss
to the happy couple, while upstairs your
dad dons plastic gloves to slide chemo capsules
down my throat. I descend for our under-eye
masks, suggest Dippity Do for your hair,
limp in Richmond's damp heat.
In your new forced-happy voice, you scream:
"Mom, I don't even,
like, know what that is!"

III. The Rappahannock River
On our cruiser the next Sunday,
Morrie's on the wheel tacking
to a broad reach, then Trevor,
middle child, a man with acres
of orchard to farm, a day job,
and two blond babies to raise,
finds my lap, his head resting
there, while I stroke his face,
touching the whisker-y wet
of his cheeks.

When I close my eyes, lift my
face to the sun, I smile at my
hairless head rising as a pearl moon,
lighting a stream of funeral food,
West Elm wedding gifts and money cards
flying to refugees, to Afghan and Ukraine
women and children, starving
but hungry for life.

Adoption

My other kids and I moaned an Irish dirge
from the hotel a hundred miles from the
crematorium, our shock and grief

salved only seconds in the sharing. Driving
home from Virginia, her boxed cinders still
hot in my hand, no autopsy, we sewed her

sweet body up tightly from town gossip,
how and why she died at 39, newly
in love, long in recovery.

I lit December's endless nights like
a desperate Druid, sweeps of white
lights reflecting inside and out,

tree-shaped altars decked with
sassy and soulful pictures
of her glowing, piles of

M&M's, chocolate kisses
bidding her to come to us
these crass Christmas days.

Earth's circling the sun nearly a
year gone now, garden turned
with her ashes, bulbs sunk deep,

waiting. I pick the plum tomatoes
lined up like teen girls huddling close
on the ground, place them on my counter,

unblemished and safe from rot,
where the black kitten who's come
here suddenly to live minces tenderly

around the vegetables, adopting us for sure,
craving my touch, my talk, her white paws
silk boots, jumping into my gait

as I walk, holding my gaze with
love and knowledge, my girl
returned.

Motherless Child

What kind of mother
would flirt on Manila's streets,
wearing her allure
light and open,
like a woven shawl,
then send me,
clutching her skirts,
knowing and not, to her own mother's home,
to the nap hammock, the mango juice,
while she pulled her lovers deeper
into her,
washing herself before my father came
home for the weekends?

Am I better? What kind of mother
would nurture her own vanity,
cling to her own black mane as
her daughter's hair vanished.
Alopecia grabbed fists of my girl's
honeyed waves until,
in her Fifth Grade Group photo,
her head appeared
as a gleaming island
of naked skin among a sea
of classmates' smiles
and mermaid curls.

In our family, mothers move
like ghosts
among their children,
then come back to life
for their grandchildren,
loving, finally, but not cured
of our childhood wounds,

that gash still oozing,
sometimes a stigmata
pouring blood.
Suffering is how I feel
special,
I learned from Opus Dei,
food and penetration
my abnegation,
though I discovered women's
tongues worked better than my boyfriend's
to make me very happy.

I wonder if my uncle
also stroked himself
in front of his younger sister,
my mother, touching her back
as he did mine,
until his milkiness spurted,
wonder what he gifted her for that.
For me, arriving in L.A.,
it was driving lessons and a room
to hang
my two dark pencil skirts,
three pale blouses suiting
my accountant's life.

Last week my mother
left forever,
hoarded her Rx's,
escaped bipolar
and debt
to leave me,
leave her five living children,
to be with Rose,

her special one.
I pry my rosary from its satin
box, a tiny coffin,
begin again the Novena.
to rescue my mother
from Purgatory,
yearning to crawl into her,
to the Virgin Mother's body,
become the beloved
fruit of her womb.

Treatment Aria

for Sue M.

When the cough fractures my focus
on Cézanne's apples and oranges—
their grace against gravity nearly
holy—we leave the Musée d'Orsay.
Landing at *Café Bohème,* I order
water and wine to clear my dry
throat, Salade Lyonnaise
to fill our bellies.

Likely the rare smoke on our Euro
holidays birthed this hack. Home,
Penn Medical's CT scan bids my
visual brain to see delicate patterns,
not non-small cell lung cancer.

Signaling I am worth saving,
I dress for immunotherapy
in high boots, chunky jewelry,
gauzy black, gray and white dresses—
chic maps of my lungs. I picture
the IV flow into my vein a cool
stream from Monet's water lilies,
X-rays later expressing the tear-shaped
tumor holding scale,
my walks from the Schuylkill to the Delaware
toughening the right lung like a fist.

Driving west, Zion's red rock
kisses cyan heavens,
Badlands' clay canyons, sand
ravines and gullies an unthinkable
moonscape, then I break into puddles,
April washing everywhere in green
at our homecoming, my white garden's

fuck-cancer tulips tall, tight waiting buds.
I work fresh dirt and summer seed
deep in our deck pots, raking them
clean at harvest.

Quebec City's reindeer and bear
sculpted in ice, snowy turrets,
our frozen breath in patisserie lines
all silver shards of joy,
till we settle deep into Christmas at home—
our tallest tree, our California girl
here, books, a fire,
stacking the Gingerbread House
sipping Sauvignon Blanc,
holding our breath, layering
the frosted roof with nonpareils,
when I touch her hair,
whisper that I am not afraid of dying:
it's just another adventure.

The Idea of Order in Idaho

after Wallace Stevens

We on the spectrum celebrated
   lockdown and quarantine as an Aspy's
     dream. Free from speech codes,

manners, the painful noise of human
   others, I hunkered down in Mom's
     and my double-wide that March,

my arts and crafts table silent
   as a Zen Garden, where I twisted grapevine
     into wreaths sprouting purple plastic fruit,

decoupaged Christmas trees, laying glitter
   thick as snowfall on green triangles.
     Come April and May, I dug deep in

my planting— by September tomatoes,
   pole beans and zukes filled our baskets—
     so on to canning. I could not return

to work, the other IT'ers talking
   about football, girls' night out,
     family reunions, sending me to

my panic place. Now I work a quiet job,
   restacking books at the local library,
     just me, my lunch bag, and my cart.

     I do try to pick up on idioms there, though,
        like *back 'atcha,* which you say *facing*
           the person's *face, team player,*

which does not refer to sports, and *baby
showers* where no one showers or even
gets wet. I write it all down.

Tomorrow, I return to my voice coach and
acting class. I don' get why the spotlight
soothes me, how I play characters when

people confuse me. But when the drama
coach says, "You're a grieving Mother.
Go!" I move her language into mine:

think of my library cart upended, garden
gobbled by critters, then I embody deep
sorrow like skin. But when she spews

director talk: multiplicity, polyphony, aesthetic
distance, I stroke my blanket swatch,
cover my ears, walk perfect squares

across the stage.

When Dumplings Open into Lotus Flowers

In Trang we woke before light
each morning,
grinding pastes
for our market sales,
pestling chiles,
dried shrimp, cumin seed
in grateful silence,
our mother's hands fragrant
with makrut lime,
cupping our faces, smoothing
our bangs before school,
bowing to remind us that only
together we make good work.

. . .

Nothing quiet about *Lemongrass,*
vibrating light and sound
14-hour days, six days a week,
goat curry stewing in coconut milk,
monkfish simmering in turmeric,
garlic and soy, trays crowded
with bird-shaped crab dumplings
lifted high on waiters' hands.
"The Most Inventive Thai Chef in the City"
chimes the NYT, though Instagram
flashes raised eyebrows at Yelp's $$$.
I post back: *Every day I turn dozens away
willing to pay that!*

. . .

Too late, my words whip around,
my mother's hissed
shame at my "I" slaps my cheek,
rubbing at my pride like a stain.

Home at my shrine
I bend prostrate,
purify crown, throat,
bring to heart center
lessons from Mommy's humility,
rhythms from my morning run.
In my third eye chakra I see
the blue lotus,
its hidden center's wisdom,
meditate on the perfection of serving,
forming chicken dumplings into blossoms
I will offer with open palms.

Moab Requiem

@reddirtpainter's
my media mojo,
though the sky pulls me
across the desert,
chasing clouds like UFO's

in my car, grabbing photos
for studio work nights
when I layer azures
on canvas mixed with
Joni Mitchell's *Blue*.

I breathe sweet sage,
ancient juniper,
watch swarms of tourists
drive through,
wanting the works with fries
while I plant my "Artist
in the Park" easel in
Arches' dry sand.

These sun-screened pilgrims
wear their wonder
open as the desert,
joy-gawk at buttes
balancing caprock spheres
as if holding their breathe
these 300 million years.

In this tourist surge,
my river and canyon curves,
plateaus scraping the sky
alive with O'Keeffe's
gorgeous ghost,
fly from the galleries.

New high-rise hotels
climb across this old
hippie town, Hyatt/Hilton's
southwest chic blocking a
tangerine sun touching
terracotta mesas.

Drought stretches into
November, Evangelists
claiming "the end of days."
Last night at Canyonland
we art girls drank to

the night snake swallowing
a lizard at our feet,
rain danced under star-scrambled
indigo, crimson wine spilling
over parched land.

No Country for Young Lawyers

Honduran killings fall like rain
on Roatan—always, on any—

grandmothers, babies, gangs.
Cartels stole our safety, kids

swept up from our stoops,
night promenades through

San Pedro Square a suicide
walk. I fled with my daughters,

this place bad for single mothers,
big firm lawyers, a price on us

all when I could not, would not
get the drug king freed from jail.

Jehovah's Witnesses flew us fast
to Philly, though my asylum papers

crawl through court like tiny turtles.
I make my own business, Lina's Cleaning,

dazzle clients with my speed, the polish
I give their kitchens, mirrors I make of

their floors. Soon I will hire workers,
rise back to the top. Cleaning makes

good cash money, more and safer than
Honduran law. I put myself in God's hands

to bless me with more work, our own home.
Still, some mornings darkness pins me

to our bed, stomps the dance in my eyes.
Then only the littlest tugging my hand for

breakfast swings my feet to the floor.
I shop Cousin's supermarket for mango,

plantain, peppers, oxtail for stew,
Pediasure for my baby to grow,

all aisles singing with Spanish,
so nice. My oldest wants Christmas,

American Girl Dolls, but I tell her
we Witness now, know Jesus did

not ask us to lay tinsel on trees,
make Feliz Navidad. Last night

I felt old fear in my dreams: from
jail, Hernandez ordered my girls

and me shot in the head, but I
rescue them from school in my

new Honda Pilot, drive us through the
air to Macy's Center City windows,

where snow falls on lanes lined
with striped candy, moving elves,

white lights lace Santa's sleigh—
pure pagan magic.

Polyamory

At Central Christian College in Kansas,
Christ's glory sundered our swollen loins
until sacred marriage would meld them.
There I loved my first husband for how much
he loved Jesus, leading us to African Mission
in Congo where the baby I caught from her
mother's bloody push, blue mottling her brown,
slippery skin, did not cry even as my fingers swept
vernix from her nose and mouth, pumped her wee
chest of fluid. Weeping, I placed her stillness
beside her mother's sobbing as God's love
seeped from me. Back in the States, I raged to
create life, midwifing my new religion, my
home birth a baptism as well in our back
yard baby pool. My then preacher husband
massaged the pain screaming through
my lower back as she crowned, Sara's
head a floating water lily, then he
lifted her from fluid to air, holding
her to the heavens. It was then I
knew I would hold holiness only
in things of this world. Adultery,
divorce wrested me from the Church's
grasp as I moved Sara and me downtown.
She sang riding the back of my bike to day
care, BLM meetings, me rocking the Philly
single mom scene, sharing both my girl with
her dad and my burning with lovers on weekends:
weed, Tinder, sex toy parties the thin red line
between my wildness and steady career climb.
Meeting marriage again on The Liberty View's rooftop,
we eye Philadelphia lit below us, our lives laden with choice:
generous love, threesomes, the sweat of activism, hard work,
children. The Bible began in God's Garden, a jail: it ends with a
shining city, fallen and free.

Interstices

Waking from the anesthetic,
starving for my life without
breasts, I asked my dad to fetch pizza,
fries, mac n' cheese, as if carbs could
replace the dead space on my chest.
Word: sacred emptiness.

'Course it's also true that I dumped
my gf soon after surgery, after she slept
by my side for days, emptying the drains
of serous fluid, queuing *Buffy the Vampire
Slayer* for our third series watch. One more
peeling off.

Been taking T for a year now, my voice
still a squawk, hoping it settles
into baritone. Moved from S2 to A2
in choir, then soloed in our concert on "I'm
Coming Out," the piano and sax crazy
on point, the house standing, clapping,
me double mic'ed and killing it.

Some days dysmorphia
follows me to the mirror,
my scars like twin smiles whispering
shame, or clubbing nights vibing Bowie
when my hips move like heavy darkness.
Yesterday, though, bare-chested, cutoffs
loose and long, I leapt for the frisbee
at Venice Beach, waved it high in the air
like a phoenix feather wand.

A Study in Posing

I hide track marks from
my parents by skin popping
between my toes, in my heel,
behind my knees.

Harder to hide from
Tri Delt Sisters on Spa Days,
Caitlyn stroking my ankle scar,
trembly voice asking me if
we should "discuss your cutting."

Today we all hit this bougie
Center City salon for beachy
balayage, our after group
selfie an embarrassment
of surfer girl posturing.
While they stuffed
their bleached smiles
away, headed back to Penn,
I stayed, wandered the Gayborhood,
dropped into the methadone clinic
for some free stuff. I do need to
study tonight.

After a weak rush and a nod,
I wake on this corner in front
of Philly Bride Boutique,
spread my backpack, books,
nuggets and fries around me,
stage my own trashy cool
Tableaux Vivant, then strike
half-lotus asana.

My view into the shop's creepy good:
a Mainline Mom in Botox
and Cartier, dead ringer for mine.
Her daughter floats from the dressing room
like some Martha Stewart Wedding model
bathed in champagne silk, beaded gloves
stretching to her toned biceps. I live to deny
Mother this costume party.

I lean toward those naked mannequins
all PoMo posed in the window,
plastic brides with creamy shoulders
and arms, staring eyeless and bald
into the future. Whatever that is.

Biker Mama Angelus

Away from Flagstar
Bank two blessed weeks
each year, Sturgis Rally's
Harley Heaven
for biker chicks—like Woodstock
but with COVID, not bad acid.
ZZ Top, REO Speedwagon & Kid Rock
at night, drinking in beer
and weed like air,
weaving through wilderness
on my Kawasaki Ninja 400,
Black Hills spires divine and dark
as Notre Dame Cathedral,
or riding ribbons of road
through gray Badlands' canyons n' craters
as if we were astronauts on the moon in '69,
awed and in love with this Blue Earth.

Millennial Cowgirl

Annie Oakley barely cleared 5' in boots—
not that I need precedent to link my stature
to cowgirl cred. I'm the lone gal here
at Teton Trail Ride, first summer away
from my family's ranch—three meals a day,
paycheck plus tips, rent-free air-conditioned camper.

But I read clients' faces when they think
we're a dump, mincing around the horse dung,
flies humming the direction to our outhouse,
so instead guests go in the woods. It's all fine by me.
Guys here treat me with respect, like one of them.
Me being petite, the long blond hair, there's little
that's butch about me, though, save my lack
of fear about much. A .45 ACP at my side,
what snake, bear or riled up boy would dare?

I like to be prepared, of course, traded my pre-law major
at Utah State (Lord knows what I was thinking back then)
for a Paramedics First Responder degree. Fits me.
I do believe, though, that I am—what did they call this
in my psychology class?—more socially and emotionally
accessible to our clientele than the guys, who can talk
roping and riding and terrain but not much else.
Me, I can stretch myself, defer to any degreed medical
professionals, sure, but since my sister's an English teacher
I can talk Hemingway and Fitzgerald to the readers,
mostly from Chicago or St. Paul, point out the season's
wildflowers—me—mostly lupine and Indian Paint, though
yesterday some real East Coaster lady lists all
that she sees—Johnson Geranium, Yarrow, Laramie Columbine,
Liatris, Arrowhead Balsamroot. So now I've tucked those
names under my touring belt.

Easier, though, to talk with westerners, other anti-vaxxers
or family values folks who appreciate knowing I come
from a Mormon-Baptist mixed marriage, religious, five kids
from 35 to 21. 'Course when I get too far into all that—
their divorces, smoking, drinking and such—even I start seeing
the contradictions, some might say hypocrisy, but as I also
know from Psych 100, people are complex. I love my family,
crazy as they are, and when my dad's in Texas, he and his
Okie brothers still oil rigging down in Galveston, I get to
be the man of the ranch, taking care of my mom a real pleasure
for me, opening doors, carrying groceries, cow punching.
No, I truly do not see myself in that whole LGBTQ+ Queer
Alliance or OUTspoken panels they sponsor at Utah State;
that's not who I am, even if I never want to marry a man
or have kids. Same for lotsa' millennial girls.

Jersey Girl

for the fierce Ukrainian people

CNN blazes blocks of buildings
shredded by Russian missiles,
only steel arches standing,

smoke snaking across rubble
like sci-fi disaster movies.
Watching bombs light

my country on fire
from our East Orange condo,
my past six-year plan

looks like vain blonde ambition:
from Kyiv to my J-1 Au Pair Visa
and job, a fast-found marriage,

Green Card, naturalization, also
nursing school. Now I witness
Kharkov apartment balconies

spew children's sleds & skates across
bombed sky, onto charred ground.
From safe America I see this.

New friends' texts crowd my phone,
sad emojis & "we're with you."
"No," whispers my gut, "you cannot be."

My family there has no heat or food
through freezing nights. Putin's mortars
explode teen flesh fleeing Mariupol,

maternity hospitals also where dark
crowns push vulvas as mothers' breasts
tear open, blood flowing like milk.

Do Americans want points
when they swarm my screen
with "Zelensky's a f'in rock star!"

What should I say to that?
Yo, ya, he's our home boy!
But when Kate MacKinnon

opened SNL with "the Ukrainian
Chorus Dumka of New York,"
sunflowers clustered in tall glass

beside girls in vyshyvanka dresses,
singing "Prayer for Ukraine,"
burning votives spelling Kyiv,

it felt like church. Not since a child
had I knelt, formed a cross
on my chest, prayed to darkness.

Gold Over America Tour

for Sylvia

Simone Biles is badass,
though my dad forbids
that talk. We're here!—
with about a billion blond,
white mamas and their daughters,
leotards tight and glittery,
acting all like Simone
and the US Women's Gymnasts
are here just for them.
Hello!—half that team black and brown girls—
Simone, Sunisa, Jordan—yeah, ladies!
Plus, lots of us black girls
in gymnastics now and at this show,
thank you very much, Ms. Biles!

Mom did my hair up in a balloon braid
ponytail, lotsa' those pink plastic spacers
clickety clacking every time I clap
and shout out, which is always,
watching this show bursting with color
and lights over floor, walls, ceiling,
waving our phones high
like so many stars,
US team, past Olympians, like Laurie Hernandez,
plus extra dancers,
big screen flashing V'ed armed landings,
flying on floor routine,
Simone nailing her Biles 2 like a hair flip,
powdery chalk on their hands for soaring
on the uneven bars and beam,
light as fairies
as if gravity's not a thing.

I suck in my breath at the finale,
praying she won't risk
the Yurchenko Double Pike Vault,
exhale when her team swarms
the floor like a band of tumbling pixies,
my mind moving to a meme
naming Simone after Tokyo
a "dying star." Really?
Guess she shines brighter now,
then, since my science teacher
says extreme energy causes
old stars to glow brightly.
"I see you,
Simon and Jordan,
Laurie and Sunisa,
I see you."

II

Team Captain & Other Poems

Team Captain

Your call to tell me
of your sentencing

was quick, like most
of your rare reaches

outward to those who've
stayed through addiction,

madness, estrangement
with you. I hear you

light a cigarette
as you say 22

to 36 months, and I
wonder what those

offenders without
fancy lawyers, trust

funds, indulgent dads
do. Ten years, often.

I can't figure
if relief or self-pity

or something like
sorrow fills the phone.

We light on what the
difference between

surviving and thriving
in state prison might

be. You always fled
and hid, an animal

from a trap, a child
beneath the bed, but

now you're found and
caught. For comfort,

I recall you gliding
the ice, faster, more

graceful than any
from the penalty box

to hustle the puck,
break away, slide

the biscuit behind
the goalie, your face

behind the bars of
your helmet smiling,

with nothing to lose.

To Be Zorro

for Rosie

I lacked, at 7,
intimacy with the gothic,
though I knew,
knocking on the door
of that lonely Victorian
on a hill,
facing a cemetery
on All Hallows Eve,
that I was out of my league.

What landed me here, in part,
was my ministry to grade school
outcasts, bound to bring them
to the safe center,
where taunts about being weird, smelly,
an eater of nose matter,
wearer of old clothes might end.

Stevie Jones was such a rescue.
More than that, small, quiet, brainy,
he was, by some yet invisible
metric, a boy from the right kind
of people, my mother declared:
shabby genteel Southerners
transplanted to our hard scrabble
town, where his grandmother
and mine
played bridge, garden clubbed,
attended Episcopal Trinity together,
recalcitrant ladies among
the women bowlers.

Though I'd declined candy cream pumpkins
collecting cat hair
on Stevie's bedside table,
I worked my pony-tailed
best at bounciness,
this friend favoring
the indoors while
I preached the pleasure of bulk candy,
dozens of sugary bribes
mounding in our sacks
outside.

I grab my kitchen broom,
black felt conical
toppling my head,
striped tights dancing
beneath a midnight velvet skirt,
my good girl turned bad witch
leading a gentle boy
aching to be Zorro
into the night,
his sheathed wooden sword,
gaucho bowler,
and black eye mask disguising
a wincing reticence.

Heading home, bags bulging with sweets,
I felt the pirates on us
from behind,
wrestling the booty
from our grip as I kicked, scratched, and bit,

Stevie brandishing his sword only
to watch it splintered over the knee
of one big kid, the second pushing
me to the ground while grabbing the spoils,
both hag and hero scrapped, bloody, scared.
After they'd left,
I searched the dry leaves
for our hats,
hoping some Halloween magic
might yet remain.

． ． ． ． ．

In high school we're still secret friends.
Stevie carries me through Chemistry,
his face wicked smart above our bubbling beakers,
my only task to type our lab reports.
I save Steve from social stigma,
lend him *Lovin' Spoonful, Vanilla Fudge*
discs, drive him to the mall
to buy the right t-shirts and jeans.

Graduation night, I come in
Magna to his Summa, later
get him high in his neighborhood
graveyard, where, stoned dramatic,
we swear we will trade hats,
Crone to Folk Hero, and back,
all our lives.

Hiking: Taos, New Mexico

Spruce top stirs
the dusk-hush.
Wings-whooshing,
air-clapping,
a Golden Eagle glides
the drop
to a parched creek bed
a mile down the canyon,
where a fox searches
for last week's slipping
stream.

We watch with uneasy thrill.
The next morning, we will return
to the bowl-bottom of Botany Trail,
find the elegant parabola
of skull and spine,
ribs still rosy with marrow,
legs gone,
tiny pinecones scattered,
auburn fur tufts brushing
this still-life.

Are We There Yet?

Straight from Glacier's
Road to the Sun, limestone
tinting mountain pools turquoise,
snow capping its peaks in July,

the drive to North Dakota features
a ten-hour study in high plains grass
the color of jaundice, sky endless
sheets of white smoke, five miles of

train cargo cars a relief from the unnerving
blankness of big sky country, even
a gas station glamorous with a place to pee,
Nutty Buddies, ten types of beef jerky

beside a stack of T-shirts promising
that if we lack deep love for the red,
white and blue, the wearer would
happily pack our suitcase for us.

When we arrive at Theodore Roosevelt
National Forest, acres of colorless
Prairie Dog Villages dust the ground,
Whack-A-Mole pups popping up and down,
waving their front paws and singing high
and strained, like the Star-Spangled Banner's
upper notes on *the land of the free,*
so high who can reach them?

What a City Has to Offer

ballooning black cloth spills   over the sidewalk   turns my head as   lifting up   from that   dark pile   a tawny rose oval a face so startling   in its perfection   I look away   then back engage with the street acknowledge her deep round eyes   brown bronze intelligent we're locked together when her hand reaches into her shirt rests on her heart then lifts her skirt points to her calves swollen giant eggplants purple tree stumps above bare feet toes gone to green grotesquery and beauty identical twins so I say I don't have cash but I'll get some for you gesture to the ATM where I am headed when it spits bills I fold her share into my pocket   check the time   remember   my punctuality goals   fly to my   pedi appointment   move her money to my wallet   my heart bloated with comforts   so I cannot return and look at her   sit instead on time   staring at my shapely feet   in the spa whirlpool before   our cash only BYOB

Odalisque

after Suzanne Valadon's The Blue Room

We get your history, babe:
Ingres' skinny girl backsides,
Manet's *Olympia* confronting us,
neither nipples
nor pubic hair to smudge
her unmarked whiteness,
more princess than queen,
sexy but not sensual,
or Picasso's *The Blue Room,*
standing woman bending
to bathe, its bedroom ghostly blues.

But your *Blue Room's*
more Lautrec's Moulin Rouge blue,
your subject, no matter her art origins,

       The Lounging Goddess of Body Positivity,

cigarette dangling, unlit,
breasts & belly bulging
against a pink cami.
green-striped silk harems
settling as a large V
pointing to her lady parts,
her face, neck & arm rosiness
signaling the same,

       Stares Sideways into the Future,
          heralds Lizzo, 2022's Athleta models,
          claims women's bodies & spirits
          sprout, settle, soar, large, lithe, round,
          stolid, willowy, curved, muscled
          escaping prescription just as you,

  Mademoiselle Mountain,
    part Target, part Dior,
    remain muse for modernity,
    postmodern poster
    shaking high & low together.
    like a cocktail.

About that blue room?
Twining white ivy on
canopy & duvet attend
you, wrap you in reading,
in sleep, in the bluest
of pleasures.

American Sonnet

after The Blue Christ
—*acrylic by Jesus Nazarenes 1985*

Suppose you look a little like Ru Paul's
Drag queens, pretty enough to know & show
Femininity as style, tropes you perform.
Suppose your granite blue shoulders, arms &
Torso slope downward like death with a six pack.
Suppose your downcast yet orbed, violet-lidded
Eyes say you're done bargaining with your
Godfather, signal you're down with the cross thing.
Your thorned crown, bound delicate
Wrists, folds of kingly purple robe just the
Romans having fun with you. Nothing personal.
Suppose you suffered, arose, got good at empire
After all. Brother Jesus, we knew, after you,
Just what you did to be so Black & Blue.

After the Fire

Jan. 5, 2022

I. The Morning Walk
My dog and I cut
a crooked path,
poke our way past
ladder trucks, police cars,
pale firehoses like jumbo
octopus arms drooping
across the street, curling
into puddles filled with fallen
bare branches
from last night's storm.

II. The News
It's not until 9,
settled home
with my coffee and laptop,
his bone, that I pull up
NBC 10 News:

13 souls woke screaming
this 6:30 am,
3 mothers and 9 children dead,
a father and his 5-year-old
child injured as they broke
second story windows filled with flame
to fall on cold concrete.

Our mayor proclaims an "immensely dark day,
worst Philly fire in over a century."
By 10, I wonder if he's counting
the 1985 MOVE inferno,
when a city SWAT team
firebombed Osage Avenue,

killing 11 "armed and dangerous"
African Americans.
Five were babies.

III. The Neighbors
By noon, recycling and trash
pickup happen on schedule,
so Nextdoor Neighbors quiet
their online complaints re:
package theft, dog feces, and litter;
instead, they mourn the dead,
Go Fund the living.

At 3 Light of the City
School staff stream rushing
lines of students into noisy,
masked order.
I open my door to watch
parents, neighbors, bus drivers
fetch kids home, backpacks
flashing Unicorn, Elsa, Spider Man
talismans.

IV. It's Always Happening
By 4 our Fairmount streets
reprise June 2020 city sounds,
when helicopters hovered
like mosquitos over our homes,
when Black Lives would not stop
going viral in death,
so, perhaps, began to matter.
Public housing the knee on the neck
this time, the "I can't breathe"

for those mothers and children
who could not afford more
room and air.

V. Grieving
By dark, we dot the steps
of their school
clutching candlelight,
throats thickening,
weary of saying their names,
the black and brown bodies burning
for centuries to escape.

VI. The Next Day
7 am ignites flame-blue,
clouds lit coral by the sun,
slipping by 10
into an ash-white sky.

Orthodox Lent

for Daria

The St. Nicholas Ukrainian Catholic Church
cradles 24th & Ringgold's corners,
gold onion dome & spires
flashing Byzantium across
our brick row homes,
giving what for
to the sun setting off
our roof decks.

These days tiny yellow & blue rectangles
twitch like prayer flags on clothes lines
across St. Nick's church garden,
vinyl signs draped
over its iron fence declaring
*Humanitarian Aid Dwindling
for Ukraine,* then a rare bid
to enter, April 8–22, 2022:
pierogis for sale.

Crossing the vestibule, I step down
in darkness to the 50s kitchen,
Formica counters lined with
thousands of potato-cabbage pillows,
dough rolled, stuffed
and packaged by aproned & stooped
congregants, my face flashing red
when the customer beside me asks
to pay with Venmo.

The half-block home
I hold my pierogies
tenderly, shaded in shame
at my pleasure in Redbud branches
twisting with plenitude,
with tight pink pods
about to explode.

My Future Memory

Will fail to lodge my failures,
Emerge elliptical, curated,
Like my mother-in-law's
And my mother's before her,
My hippocampus a dried porcini
Breeding blithe hubris.

Only my shining moments will survive.
My children must witness
My embarrassment of admirers,
The plants and cards crowding my downsized space
A mere sampling, I assure them,
Of gifts appearing on my birthday.
Stories about my youthful beauty will surface—
Those waitresses who often mistook me for my son's date!
Or more restaurant tales:
A chicken chunk lodged in an old man's throat
That I Heimliched across tables,
Diners' gaping, then clapping.
I need wait only minutes
Before I deliver
My identical brags again,
And even again.

Will it happen gradually for me,
Or all at once?
Or perhaps, God forbid, not at all.
Will I be doomed to remember?
So that every night when I wake to pee
I am haunted by times I drunkenly offended—
"Bitch" and "dick" jabbed at friends—
Fucked my graduate TA,
Prayed for the receding hairline of my husband's ex-

To migrate further to the back of her head,
Stuffed a neighbor's mailbox with dog shit,
Offering her empathy, vowing to help
Catch the culprit?

Quarantine Cuisine

Lockdown-contained, travel-curtailed, my chef brain leaps to compensate, wanders cage-free, up and out of former meal rotations—Chicken Piccata, Pasta Puttanesca, mustardy pork loin partnered and roasted with fingerlings and brussels: though lovely, these culinary participants in a previous cooking life got pink-slipped fast, registering the CEO's reconfigured vision, menus finally going all out free-range, or more like Girls Gone Wild, me wearing not a wet T-shirt, of course, but dirty-aproned? yeah, baby, each week ringing my 88-year-old neighbor's doorbell, bearing lamb shank tagine traveling from Morocco, simmered with dates and couscous, or Nigerian Peanut and Pumpkin soup dolloped out the wazoo with creme fraiche, chopped chives, but really making him smile, finally, with Italian Potato Pasta Soup, me explaining over city traffic noise how often, really, Northern Italians double-team these starches in a single dish, cut them with wilted dark greens and lemon, pile on a parmesan cloud before serving, his expression as he reaches for the pot signaling "I don't give a rat's ass." When I deliver a Thai Curry with silky tofu and jammy tomatoes, this Korean war vet declares that only the Red Chinese believe it's a dinner without meat, but I don't quibble over the nationality of my broth's Asian descent (though wonder later if I should've), as Christmas Cookie Palooza is upon us, trending international as well; this year, losing the Hershey Peanut Blossoms, Spritz, Pecan Tassies—tribute sweets to my deceased mother— whirring my Kitchen Aid Artisan 5 Quart 24/7, fueled by a commitment to cover at least five continents, turning out Piparkakut, Chinese Peanut Cookies, Russian Chocolate Kolbasa, Raspberry Rose Rugelach, Australian Anzac Biscuits, Dolce de Leche Thumbprints, then boxing them with starry tissue, It's a Small World After All (sorta') logos on the sides, anticipating Carl's nationalist sneer, though when he opens the door to me Christmas Day, hears this year's deviations, I feel his arms around me, accept my yearly poinsettia, decipher through his mask the words: "I like that. The world's all in this Chinese virus together, toots."

Ode to the Christmas Cactus

Across the world we haul conifers
Indoors, honor Celts' trees torched on
Winter nights, blaze ours, as well, with current,
White light, sacrament of this century
To ancient, dark gods.
In this pine and spruce season,
Why lay the ledge with succulent's
Clawed arms, mix yuletide boughs,
Alpine's fragrant firs, with December's
Crimson cactus flowers?

Those faithful to Luke Two's hagiography,
(As well as textual geography),
Cite camels desert driven toward The Star,
Three kings, late, gifts borne to the child,
Find Christ's masse holy with arid blooms.
Well, then.

In fact, this plant's Brazilian born.
Its aerial roots search Amazon's trees,
Heliotroping towards rainforest's roof,
Yearning, like us all, for bangles of light.
Though North's sun dozes through midwinter,
Cactus mouths will open, pink pistils tonguing
Epiphany's air, this epiphyte
Trumpeting, in magna canta laughing:
Gloria, gloria, in excelsis blooming!

Notes

"Preface: On Not Staying in My Lane": The quotations from Rekdal are from her book, *Appropriate: A Provocation* (2021), 90–91. References to Pamela Paul and Henry Louis Gates, Jr. are excerpted, respectively, from "The Limits of Lived Experience," NYT, April 24, 2022, and "Literary Freedom as an Essential Human Right," Oct. 12, 2021.

"No Country for Young Lawyers": Juan Antonio Hernandez is a convicted Honduran drug trafficker, lawyer, and politician. He is the brother of the former President of Honduras, Juan Orlando Hernandez.

"Are We There Yet?": The last lines of the poem intentionally echo Belize's monologue about America from Tony Kushner's two-part play, *Angels in America: A gay Fantasia on American Themes* (1991).

"Odalisque": I recently encountered French artist Suzanne Valadon for the first time at a Barnes Art Museum show of her work in Philadelphia, Fall 2021, titled *Suzanne Valadon: Model, Painter, Rebel*. The very fact that a major painter of the modernist period, financially successful and celebrated throughout her lifetime, had been buried in obscurity for a century illustrates the sexism and male dominance prominent in the western art world for centuries.

"American Sonnet": The last lines of the poem intentionally echo lines from the Louis Armstrong performance song, "What Did I Do to Be So Black & Blue?" Ralph Ellison includes this phrase as well in his pastiche Prologue to his novel, *Invisible Man*.

About the Author

VA Smith is a former Penn State University, College of Liberal Arts Excellence in Teaching instructor of English. She founded Philadelphia's Chancellor Writing Services, where she served as a writing coach for over a decade. Currently, VA hones her poetic rhythms walking and biking, serves as a home chef/caterer, and loves on her friends, family, partner, Peloton, and dog.

VA has dropped poetry into dozens of literary journals and anthologies, among them: *Blue Lake Review, Calyx, Evening Street Review, Ginosko Literary Journal, MacQueen's Quinterly, Oyster River Pages, Pure Slush's Lifespan Volumes, Quartet, Southern Review, Third Wednesday, Verdad,* and *West Trade Review*. Kelsay Books published her first poetry collection, *Biking Through the Stone Age,* in 2022.

Currently, she's working on a third collection of travel poems, titled *Elsewhere.*

www.ingramcontent.com/pod-product-compliance
Lightning Source LLC
Chambersburg PA
CBHW071012160426
43193CB00012B/2019